HOW I'VE GROWN TO KNOW TRUE LOVE

BY

Terry La-shon Riley

Bloomington, IN Milton Keynes, UK

AuthorHouse™
1663 Liberty Drive, Suite 200
Bloomington, IN 47403
www.authorhouse.com
Phone: 1-800-839-8640

AuthorHouse™ UK Ltd.
500 Avebury Boulevard
Central Milton Keynes, MK9 2BE
www.authorhouse.co.uk
Phone: 08001974150

© 2006 Terry La-shon Riley. All rights reserved.

No part of this book may be reproduced, stored in a retrieval system, or transmitted by any means without the written permission of the author.

First published by AuthorHouse 4/6/2006

ISBN: 1-4259-2671-1 (sc)

Printed in the United States of America
Bloomington, Indiana

This book is printed on acid-free paper.

Acknowledgments

First and last of all, I would like to give thanks to God, my heavenly father, for giving me the wisdom, knowledge, and strength to communicate my words through writing, in hopes that it will truly inspire someone that has gone through similar or the same situations. Second, also I would like to give thanks to one of my favorite people in the world, and that is my mother, Alberta Williams, for inspiring and encouraging me to do what I have done when I was going through my trials and tribulations. When things didn't seem bright in my life, she was there for me. I would also like to thank my spouse, Michael Riley, for being a patient husband, plus a friend, and for cheering me on while I was writing my book. I would also like to thank my oldest son, for supporting me and helping me put the finishing touches on my story. Last of all, I would like to thank my niece Tyrenda Little for patiently listening to me while I was writing my book. Thank you all for your support and love. May God bless you all!

Love,
Terry Riley

I don't know any other way to say this but life can be a real bitch sometimes! Well, it all started with me, as we say back in the day. I'm talking early '80s, of course. By the way, excuse me for not properly introducing myself. I'm known as Anita, but my nickname is "Newkie." Ask me how I got the nickname. I don't know, but I learned to live with it. Well, getting back to my story, I was only fourteen years old when I met what you might call my first love. He was a fair-looking, brown-skinned guy, with muscles and a little bit of this and a little bit of that, if you know what I mean. I adored this young man, who was two years older than me and who made me feel loved. Not to say that I wasn't given love by my family, of course. I've always had a loving family and a mother who's always been there for me, through "thick 'n' thin," but this particular time I should have listened to my mother. They have always said Momma knows best. I was heading for heartache down the road, but who would have known that. Things were really picking up with this relationship I was deeply involved in. A girl my age should have been more focused on graduating high school and college, not being married at such a young age. When I think back, things were moving a little to fast; also looking back on my life, so to speak, who could have of known that things would have turned out the way that they did? I never would have imagined this man whom I once called my soul mate and my best friend would have hurt me the way he did. It all started when Derrick, my first husband, the man I shouldn't have married, and me had our first child. But anyway too late for the "I told you so." There I was, this young, beautiful girl married at the age seventeen and a half. I thought I pretty much knew it all. What was my rush? I didn't get married because I was pregnant, but because I thought I had finally found someone who truly loved me, because I truly loved him just as much. When our son came along (his name, by the way, is Jamal and he's the cutest little baby you can imagine having in your life), the timing wasn't right. We were both separated and lived at home with our own parents. It wasn't the kind of family you would call picture-perfect; in fact, it was an embarrassing situation for me at that time. I always felt a couple, especially one with a child, should be in their own place; at least that's how I was raised.

Derrick wasn't the kind of husband who would rub my stomach or my feet when I was having aches and pains throughout my pregnancy. He was cold as ice toward me. He made me feel as though he was allergic to women that were pregnant: he avoided me. I can't even recall him doing anything special for me throughout my pregnancy; all I wanted was a little pampering from him, but instead I got served the third degree!

What happened to the man I thought was once my prince charming? He was like someone else out of Invasion of the Body Snatchers. Things just weren't looking too good for us, so I decided to move up north, near more of my kinfolk. I took my child and got the hell out of town. I knew it was time for me to move on and start a new life somewhere else. I just wasn't happy anymore with this man I was married to; he ran around on me with different women and treated me like the dirt underneath his shoe. But it was up to me to make that change, and change I did. Finally my son and I were in our own place far away from this man, who called himself my child's dad, even though our son was too young to realize what a dad was; but I knew the deal, and all that came with it, of course. He was full of it. I was now living in a new state, trying to start my life over, until one day I got bad news that my grandmother had passed away. She was sickened with cancer, God bless her soul. She was a lovely lady and will be truly missed by her whole family. Anyway, I had an older sister who lived nearby. Her name is Eva; she can be very envious at times, especially toward me. I could never figure out why she never cared for me. As far back as I can remember, ever since I was a little girl I felt she had it in for me. I never felt our sister's relationship had blossomed, but had died somewhere along the way. I thought when I moved away to be near my oldest sister, Eva, and family members, things would possibly change for the better; but instead things became even uglier between us. As time went on, my feelings for her started to change, not by choice but by the constant bullshit I was being put through by her over the years. Finally, I woke up one morning and I was in my new home being the responsible mother that I am, taking care of my child and my business. But something inside me knew it wasn't quite right to treat the father of my child as if he didn't exist in my world any longer. I wished I was waking up from a bad dream, but I couldn't deny the fact that this child of mine might grow up to resent me because I kept his father completely out of his life for my own selfish reasons. So I did it! I made the phone call after three months of not telling Derrick where I was staying. I broke the silence by letting him speak with his child, only to prove that I didn't have to be the monster that he once was to me. At that particular moment he wanted to ask me how I was doing, and truthfully, at the time I was not so good because I had just lost my grandmother a few days earlier. I believe he then used that as a weapon to play on my emotions; he not only wanted to take part in my grandmother's funeral but he also mentioned the fact that he missed his son and wanted to see him soon as possible. Honestly, if it weren't for my grandmother's funeral, I might have told him to wait a little longer, as far as seeing his son. Don't forget I was still heated up from the mess he had put me through. Eventually Derrick made his way up north to be with his son, Jamal, and attend my grandmother's funeral. Prior to his arrival, the deal was to just stay briefly for no longer than one week. For some particular reason, I found myself lured back into his trap; of course, he did everything in his power to make me want him all over again. He tried being everything that he never once was to me. Basically he did things that I had longed for over the years. I found myself falling back in love with him again, and I didn't mean for it to happen. The fact is he is the father of my child, and I always wanted Derrick to be a part of my child's life instead of a man that wasn't Jamal's biological father. Somewhere in my mind I knew it wouldn't work, but part of me wanted to believe he had changed. Derrick had asked me to take him back and I kind of felt the need to in order to make my family work. I thought my moving away had hopefully made him see the light. Well, eventually one week led to two weeks; then three, and four, and before I knew it Derrick was permanently back in my life. Derrick came up for a visit only to find himself living with me; he knew no one else but me and most of my relatives, whom he had met on several visits. He had made the decision to stay with me and never return to the South to live. He lived off me and I took very good care of this man while he searched for a job high and low. While in the process, I got pregnant with his child once more. Big mistake! What the hell was I thinking about after the hell he had once put me through? I should have known better than to let this happen again. I don't regret that my child was born, but whom he was going to be born by. How could I have been so stupid, knowing that I had been previously treated as if I did not exist? When I mentioned to Derrick that I was pregnant with his second child, he became very angry about it; he seemed to be more worried about paying child support than about me keeping the baby that was growing inside me. I knew at that point that he was going to be unsupportive toward me like he had been in the past. It was nobody's fault but mine for even allowing him to impregnate me again.

He was strongly against it. I knew he didn't want me to keep the baby, but it was my body, not his. I felt he could care less about what a woman had to go through to get rid of a baby. By that time I was going on six weeks, and he still couldn't accept the fact that I was going to go through with my pregnancy. He had finally landed a job, working for an insurance company around mostly Caucasians, and for no particular reason, I believe this black man who once grew up in the same home town as me had lost his roots. I know that there weren't many black people working at the same place of employment, so I guess he felt the need to act as if he was a white man instead of a black man in order to fit in with his co-workers. He would come home from work and act like his ass was some type of king on a throne. He got so beside himself I don't even think he knew who he was anymore. He started to look down on me, as though I wasn't good enough for him. I was a stay-at-home mom on disability. I wasn't quite able to work due to my situation. I suffered from what you would call an anxiety disorder. I had to struggle with it most of my adult life. Most people don't quite understand what it means, but I can tell you this much: it doesn't mean that you're crazy. This illness was something I found quite difficult to talk about for many years, but just like anything else, you learn to live with the things that life can unexpectedly throw at you.

Anyway, enough talk about me. Derrick had gotten so totally out of control; he would call from work just to tell me that he wouldn't be coming home for a few hours because he and his co-workers were going over to the bar to play pool. Don't get me wrong: this man had been at work all damn day, but I was stuck in the damn house taking care of our son and child to be, cooking and cleaning all day. I also forgot to mention going through terrible morning sickness. The least he could have done was check in on his family first. No, not him; he had to have things his way. Don't get me wrong: I believe in giving a man his space, but in this case if you were to give Derrick an inch, he would take a mile. Basically he was inconsiderate when it came down to respect. Eventually things between Derrick and me started to fall apart; we were always arguing over the stupidest things, especially with him wanting to hang out all of the time. He really was irking my nerves, and with me being pregnant this didn't help at all; it just made my anxiety level go up higher. I can recall having an argument with Derrick, which was the last straw that broke the camel's back. In the heat of the argument, he spit on me and he threatened to throw me down the stairs, and of course, this had sent me into a rage. I put his ass out of my home. I felt I was better off living by myself than dealing with a man whom I felt would soon cause me to miscarry if I continued on the way I was going. Peace finally! At last there was peace in my home. I admit, for some odd reason I still felt something for this man. I didn't want to, but I guess it was only natural to feel a little something; after all, he was still my husband. So some time had gone by since I had last seen Derrick; we hadn't spoken in several months. But I had gotten word from a close friend of mine that he had been seen in town with another woman; and not only had he been seen in town, but he also had gotten his own place. I didn't want to believe it at first, but something seemed strange about the whole thing. I knew it wasn't like Derrick not to come around and snoop or make up some kind of lame excuse, when in fact he would try to use his son as an excuse just to see what I was doing. Things had gotten very quiet for sometime. I was starting to reach my seventh month. While walking outside of my home one day, on my way to my doctor's appointment, I happened to see my husband, Derrick, driving around the complex that I live in, with a car that, of course, belonged to an ex-girlfriend of his who lived back home. Boy did I become angry! Out of all the things this man had put me through, you would at least think he would have had the decency not to bring his mess around me, trying to show off something that wasn't even his just to get me jealous. As he drove by, he looked at me with this smirky look on his face, as though I was to break down and cry. I admit it hurt me, but I wouldn't give him the satisfaction of seeing me break down. I then knew at that point that he was back to his no-good ways. I thought to myself as I drove off for my doctor's appointment, "What kind of woman could be that stupid and desperate to want to be involved with a man who was still married and who had a child?" The saddest thing about it was he also had a baby on the way. I was curious to see if this girlfriend of his was really staying with him, because if so, I felt she had a lot of nerve to bring her no-good sorry ass up to the town where I was living. I know it must sound crazy that I'm carrying on this way, but my hormones were raging out of control, and one thing you don't want to do is cross a woman when she is pregnant. How could this woman, who was now living with my husband, be so naive about the rebound that was taking place right before her very own eyes? You would think that she would have been intelligent enough to tell him to work out his problems with his wife first, and then call her back when he became a free man. No, not her; she must have thought her ass was made out of solid gold, until one day he decided to show her his true colors, which he definitely did indeed. The next thing I knew she packed up her things and headed back home. We named our second child Shavon; he was an eight-pound-two-ounce baby. He was adorable with that cute little dimple on the side of his right cheek. I had forbidden Derrick from coming up to the hospital to see his son; he didn't deserve to be anywhere near me and his child. After all, he was against me having his child. But for some strange reason, Derrick found out I had given birth to his son. Of course, my big-mouth sister, Eva, had to call him up and tell him which hospital I was staying at. I was shocked to see him walk through the doors of my room; he acted as though he had always been a part of my and my child's lives. How could this man act like nothing ever happened? I felt at that moment that I could just jump right out of my bed and strangle his damn neck and squeeze out any life remaining inside of him. I found out later from the hospital that he had pretended to be one of my brothers in order to get up to my room. Well, anyway, that day at the hospital had passed and other days had followed; the kids were growing up into young men; and I couldn't carry on being married to a man who wasn't being a full-time father but a part-time dad and a wannabe husband, if he wasn't out somewhere screwing around. I knew that it was time for our marriage to come to an end. I hated myself for staying married to this man as long as I did. I wish someone had locked me up in a room, chained me down, and didn't release me until I finally came to my damn senses about how this man was clearly a waste of my time. No! I had to be hard headed and stubborn, and learn things the hard way. As time went on we both were finally divorced. Derrick had started seeing this woman by the name of Cynthia; she was trouble in the making, but this time Derrick had gotten a taste of his own medicine. He had finally found his match. He thought as always that he had this woman eating out of the palm of his hand, but to his surprise she was the type who didn't stand for any bullshit. He was dating a woman who would soon turn his world upside down. But all the while he was using her on the rebound because of our recent breakup. He must have thought when he ended the relationship with Cynthia that she would take it gently, but instead she hollered rape and went down to the police station and gave them a show about how this black man she didn't want to let go of had raped her, pulled out a gun on her, and threatened to kill her if she told anyone. I can recall that day, at home in my bedroom, sitting on the edge of my bed, expecting a phone call from Derrick as usual about him picking up his kids; but for some strange reason I didn't get my usual call, so I started to call around to find out what was going on with him. I got in my car and drove over to my ex-husband's house. I went to knock on the door and I got no answer. Finally I got back into my car. I was sitting there in his driveway, wondering where the hell he could be, thinking who could be more important than his own kids; thinking he had ditched his kids to go and hang out with one of his no-good hoes. As I went to turn the ignition, my car wouldn't start, for some odd reason; it was like maybe God was trying to tell me something. Then out of nowhere came this man up behind my car, knocking on the window trying to get my attention. He replied by saying that earlier that day, Derrick was arrested and taken into custody at the police station. I raced on over to the police station to see what was going on. When I arrived there, Derrick was behind bars looking frantic as hell; he had the look of fear in his eyes. You could just smell the fear once you entered into his lockup. He looked at me as though he had seen an angel coming to rescue him from all his worries. But reality had suddenly kicked back in; he knew I wasn't above the law to do such a thing. As he spoke to me with a trembling voice I could hear how frightened he was; he needed my help desperately. I believe even after all the shit he had put me through he made it obviously clear that he was now at my mercy. I guess at that particular moment it felt good to see a man of such strength become so weak. I then knew that the tables were finally turning. He seemed too overwhelmed to speak; he didn't know where to start. He tried his best to convince me that he was not guilty of raping this so-called girlfriend of his. He at this point needed me to make some important phone calls for him; he needed me to get a lawyer. "Why me?" I said to myself. He also needed me to reach his family, who had no idea what was going on. I felt in my heart the need to help him, but at the same time I could have stabbed him in the damn back for all the unnecessary bullshit he had put me through countless times.

This could have been the perfect time to make him suffer and feel the pain that he had once placed upon me. I hated him so much I would have enjoyed torturing him, but my heart and soul wouldn't allow me to be that kind of person. I wanted so much to hurt him the way that he hurt me.

As we talked to each other about how he needed me to help him, my mind suddenly went back into a flashback of how this man had hurt me over the years. I could seriously see how much pain he was in. He was depending on me to be there for him; he didn't have any family around other than me. The only thing separating us were the iron bars between us, and I knew that I could have simply walked away, leaving him to squirm like a rat in a cage, or I could have been the kind and forgiving woman I am by extending my hands to him and helping him even if I felt he didn't deserve it. Had I gone mad? Or was I just being a plain fool for this man once more? Well, that day when I got back home, I pulled out the yellow pages in desperate need of an attorney. For God's sake, it was the weekend, Saturday afternoon; everything was practically closed, but finally after one more attempt, there was this man on the other end of phone saying, "Can I help you?" I couldn't believe my ears: someone had finally picked up the phone. Was it just luck on his side, or simply God giving him the chance to be heard? I proceeded by saying, "My ex-husband needs your help. He was accused of raping someone; he needs someone to represent him quickly or he could soon lose his job and possibly go to jail for a long, long time." So there I was, trying to save this man's future, which was at stake, but a tiny voice in my head kept saying, "He is going to hurt you again, just you wait," but I kept ignoring it because I knew that I wouldn't.

How I've Grown to Know True Love

Having been successful at trying to help him in the situation at hand, all I could think about was my poor kids are growing up in the world without a father in their lives. So I guess that is what really motivated me do what I had to do to keep my kids' father from being incarcerated. There I was, Anita being a host to his family, who arrived at my home in support of their son. I had completely opened up my home to this ex-family of mine, knowing that in the past they hadn't always treated me so nice. We had our quarrels and disagreements in the past while Derrick and I were dating back in high school. I don't believe they cared much for me because of my upbringing. I felt that they thought of me as this stuck-up princess who was too good for their son. Well, even after all that drama between both our families we still managed to be civil to one another anyway. As the night approached, there was Derrick ringing my phone off the hook, needing someone to talk to, when, of course, I probably would have been his last choice; but he knew that no one probably would have been foolish enough to let him run up their phone bill by accepting his constant collect calls. I must have been foolish enough, because I let him do it to me. He would call me all different times of the day and I would try to console him by letting him know that I was doing everything to help get him out of jail. I knew that he was sending my phone bill sky high every time I accepted his phone calls, but he promised me that when he got out that he would pay for my phone bill. Like I really believed that shit! He barely wanted to pay child support. Also, I forgot to mention his family and my mom had finally gotten his ass out on bail. He came to live with me because he had been evicted from his apartment and he had no place else to go. People were talking about it all over town, and the friends he thought he had were no where to be found. While awaiting his trial, he was like a changed man: he wouldn't leave the house much; he spent most of his time with me and the kids. The front page of the paper was blasting his name and previous address all over the place, as though they had nothing better to do. Yes, we were living in a predominately white town, with very few black people, so to them it was like repeating the O. J. Simpson case over and over again. They rarely had anything major go on in town, so to them this was like a breath of fresh air, something for them to talk about: a black man had finally gotten some publicity. Derrick's self-esteem was so low he didn't know what to do; he didn't think the same people he once worked with and thought were his friends would so soon remind him of how he was not white but black. Their attitudes toward him were very different now that he was awaiting trial; he didn't know how to trust anymore, so he said. He even mentioned to me that he could never, ever date another woman, especially a white woman, because of how hurt he was. He felt the only woman he could trust was me; he now knew for sure that I was the woman for him. He said that he never should have treated me so badly. He admitted to all his wrongdoings, and, what shocked me, the man had the nerve to propose marriage to me all over again; and of course, I knew it was just fear talking, not really Derrick. Well, anyway, Derrick's trial had arrived and there was me, Anita, his ex-wife, up on the witness stand, trying my best to protect this man from possibly going to prison. Now how many women do you know would go on the witness stand for an ex-husband? Normally the ex would have been on his own in this case especially after the bullshit he had put me through over the years. Derrick didn't seem so tough now, when indeed he knew his life was hanging by a thread and could easily be snipped at any given moment. As I sat on the witness stand, I could see fear written all over his face as the sweat rolled from his nervous body. I kind of felt that no human being should have to go through what he had to go through, especially if he or she were being wrongfully accused. Out of all the things Derrick and me had been through over the years, I didn't think he was capable of raping someone. I knew he could be nasty and even cruel with some of his ways, but for God's sake, not a rapist. The trial went on for about one week before they reached a verdict; he was soon relieved of his anxieties. He was pronounced a free man. Boy that was close! I said to myself, "Just waiting for the verdict can frighten someone to death," literally speaking. Finally! I felt we were able to move on with our lives and somehow be a family even though I knew things still wouldn't quite be the same after that frightening day. Slowly but surely, Derrick was changing back into his old ways as though he never stopped. I found myself seeing his change take place over time, a change that would make you wonder, if this situation didn't change him then what would? I went to my mother, whom I often go to at times for guidance and advice. It was killing me inside to ask the question that most people probably would ask: "Do you think he would change on me again like he did in the past? After all, I stuck by his side through all of his hurt while awaiting trial, and the least he could do is keep his word to me."

My mother responded by saying to me, "Give him enough rope to hang himself. Time will tell; time always tells." I never forgot the words my mother had spoken, for surely there would come a day when Derrick would break my heart for the last time. After that day I promised myself that I wouldn't let another man hurt me anymore the way that he did. Once again, there I was living my life alone with my two sons. Derrick and I had moved on with our lives; he eventually started seeing this white woman that he worked with on his job. When he came around to pick up his sons, he would always have something negative come out of his mouth, and his favorite word would be bitch, if for some reason we would get into an argument about the kids. He would pull up in front of my house as though he thought he was something else, just because he had a white woman on the side of him looking back at me as though she thought she had taken the black man from me. Honestly, I was happy to see him finally go on with his life, but I felt sorry for this woman, who had no idea what she was dealing with. Derrick was a user, and I knew soon it was just a matter of time before she would get a taste of what he was really all about.

One day while at the Laundromat, I met this white man by the name of Steve; he was very charming and handsome. He came up to me and introduced himself to me, and at that time I was busy trying to get my family back on track after all the things we had been through. He found me to be very attractive and wanted to take me out on a date. I wasn't really interested in dating at that time, but he would always call me and ask me to go out with him, so finally one day I went out on a date with him. It was wonderful! We continued to see one another; it soon turned into a serious relationship, and at that point I felt if I was going to be dating this man, it was only proper to introduce him to my kids' father. So one day when Derrick came to pick up the kids, he seemed shocked to see me with this white man who stood very tall and handsome. Derrick looked as though he couldn't believe his eyes. I think Derrick must have thought that he was the only one capable of being in a biracial relationship. Derrick stared Steve up and down, as if he didn't care for him. I introduced Derrick to Steve while walking up to my doorway. There was Steve sitting on my front porch looking like he didn't have a clue about what was going on between the two of us. Steve went to shake Derrick's hand, and Derrick drew his hand back as though he didn't want to accept the fact that I for sure was now moving on with my life. Derrick stood there in a daze, as though he had forgotten what he had originally come there for. I finally called out his name and Derrick took a deep breath as though he had to collect himself and not let on to me that the situation at hand was now affecting him more than I thought it would. Derrick finally gathered himself together and drove off with the kids for the weekend. As last I had gotten that part of my life out of the way. I knew then that the only thing left now was to focus on the new relationship that was starting to develop between me and Steve. Soon thereafter, there came a day when Steve would propose marriage to me, and of course, I accepted his proposal. I never felt, after the relationship with Derrick, that I would ever be in a serious relationship again with anybody else; not only that, but I also felt that being with Steve had opened my eyes to how a woman should really be treated. Steve treated me so good that it made me wonder how in the hell I ever tolerated my ex-husband as long as I did. I was just so happy and in love with this man I had married; he was like a breath of fresh air to me, giving me the chance to rid myself of all the bad pollution that was still bundled up inside of me from over the years. I was able to breathe again! I hadn't felt like this in years. It felt like a load had been taken off of me. Steve was the kind of husband that would trust me with just about anything that was his, even his wallet. When he got paid on pay day, he would come home from work and give me his wallet to hold, and tell me that I could buy whatever I wanted just as long as I left enough money in his wallet to pay the bills. Steve basically treated me like a queen. Steve was very different from the average husband; most husbands wouldn't dare allow their wife to be in control of their belongings. Steve didn't mind doing sweet things for me. Steve felt that if you were to be in a marriage to someone, it meant trusting them fully, or what was the point of even being married? That's what I liked about Steve: he didn't care about what other men thought, he believed in pleasing his spouse. My ex-husband, Derrick, would never have been as generous to me as Steve was; in fact, he would have called him henpecked and a faggot for just being the kind of husband he was to me. As time went on, there was Derrick coming by the house as usual to pick up the kids on his weekends. When he saw how good Steve was treating me, he would make stupid remarks about my new husband, saying that he believed he was gay! Just because he wasn't running around on me.

Derrick was jealous to see another man treat me like a queen, because he did the total opposite. I would often tell Derrick the one that you suspect is gay may be the one he's with. He would only laugh and say, "Yeah, right!" He must have thought that his girlfriend was so into him that there was no possible way she would be interested in another woman. But as time went on, Derrick and his girlfriend started to have major problems. He would call me up and ask me to keep the kids on his weekend because his girlfriend, whom he was staying with, would get mad with him during an argument and would threaten to throw him out of her home. Finally there came a day when Derrick and his girlfriend had completely broken up with one another. They both worked at the same job, which, of course, made it difficult for them to keep their personal business away from the job. Somehow everyone on the job would find out about everything that went on in their relationship; everyone pretty much knew their business, especially when his ex-girlfriend started seeing another woman on the job. Derrick was so humiliated and embarrassed that this so-called woman he had been dating had gone as far as to hurt him by dating a co-worker who was bisexual like her, and who sat right in the same cubicle with both of them. The truth had finally come out: she no longer cared about how she was making a fool out of herself and Derrick. The situation on their job had gotten out of hand with them bringing their personal problems from home onto the job, which soon caused them both to be terminated from their jobs. Steve and I had stayed married for a short period of time. I really would like to think that Steve was a wonderful, loving husband who would do just about anything to make you happy, except for one or two things: he was too busy trying to please his older sister, whom he looked to as a mother figure. Supposedly as a child she helped raise him while growing up because his mother wasn't always around to help him; she was busy working most of the time. Steve felt it was important to have his older sister's approval when he needed it. Steve soon started having problems with my two sons, who at times I admit could really work up a pair of nerves. They started to give my new husband a hard time, and I believe Derrick had been working on the kids to have them show dislike toward my new husband,

Steve, because he didn't want to see me happy. Steve eventually got to the point that he was no longer able to deal with my kids' behavior, "so he says." I honestly feel that his sister played a part in our marriage coming to an end; there were certain things that went on between his sister and me. I can recall a time when we were sitting at my kitchen table, and she had threatened me by saying that if she wanted to, she could stop her brother from being with me, a statement I found to be very offensive. I knew then that she was definitely out to destroy our relationship.

If for some particular reason she didn't like something that went on in our marriage, she would definitely show it toward her brother and me, as though we had to have her approval on things. I truly believe she didn't like the fact that her brother was married to a black woman, with an already-made family and, of course, a previous marriage history. But that I felt wasn't her call; she should have just minded her own business and let her little brother, Steve, live his own life. Instead, she wanted to find faults in our marriage, when there were plenty of faults in her own relationship she could have been working out instead of putting her nose where it didn't belong. After my second divorce to Steve, I was really afraid of marriage at that point. I felt that maybe I wasn't cut out for it. Every time I turned around, it seemed like I was right back where I had started, and that was single. I thought to myself that maybe there wasn't a man out there good enough for me. I needed someone who could really love me for me, and understand me through and through. I would pray to God to please send me a man that hopefully wouldn't break my heart anymore. I would also ask God to let him be a little bit older than me and be ready to settle down with a woman who has always put God first in her life; and it was very important that he go to church and love kids. I made it a point to start putting God first in my life, and definitely when it came down to making crucial decisions about me being with someone again. I realized that what I wanted wasn't always the best thing for me, but what God had planned for me was better for me. So I learned to wait patiently on the Lord, for I knew that he couldn't do me any wrong; at least that's what the Bible said. I knew in my heart that one day God would bless me with that type of man, if I only believed it. I got sick and tired of running into men that weren't for me. My first husband I married too young, and I was warned about him. My second husband I married because I thought to myself if I didn't marry this man, I probably wouldn't marry again. But I'm much older and wiser now, and my mother always said to me that when God gets ready he will put someone in your life, and when he does you will know it. I always heard growing up as a child that God won't give you someone that will waste your time, but who will love you for you and treat you the way you ought to be treated, and it won't last a minute or a second but a lifetime. So two years after Steve and I had been divorced, I met my future husband, Michael. One day while passing my apartment, Michael looked at me with a gleam in his eyes; it was like love at first sight. This man couldn't stop looking back at me while driving by. He would often drive by and wave to me, as though he already knew me. We both were neighbors; we lived in the same complex as each other. I would sometimes bump into Michael at the grocery store, and we would chit-chat about whatever. I knew there was something special about this man: he stood six feet one, with broad shoulders, and his complexion was the color of chocolate milk. When he smiled, he would light up the whole room. He had such a beautiful smile that seeing him smile made you want to smile back at him. One day I got a knock on the door, and when I opened it there was Michael, standing there looking like a little boy. On our first date, all I can remember was him holding this porcelain elephant in his hands, asking me to have it as a gift. Michael knew I liked elephants; I collected them and added the one he gave me to my collection. I was really surprised to see how much he paid attention to what I liked; I believe he heard me at the supermarket say something about having a collection of elephants on my shelf at home. I was amazed at how he paid close attention to the fine details of our little conversations, here and there, in passing one another in the grocery store. While standing there in my doorway, he mentioned to me that he would like to take me out on a dinner date. He stood there as though he was expecting me to say no! But I said yes, what the heck. I couldn't remember the last time I'd gone out on a date since my last divorce. For some reason I felt good about accepting his invitation to dinner. I had a strange feeling that I had never had before, but I knew it was a good feeling. Shortly after that, Michael and I saw each other from time to time. I was being very careful about taking our relationship slow; I didn't want to rush into anything too fast. I guess I was just making sure I didn't repeat the same mistakes all over again. I wanted so badly to trust this man called Michael, but it seemed like my heart just wouldn't let me love the way I wanted to love someone. When I went to bed at night I would always pray that God would send me a good man who wouldn't break my heart into a million pieces. I actually felt at times that I didn't have any more heart to be broken, but I knew that was just foolish thinking on my part.

Michael one day popped the big question: he had asked me if I would marry him. We had been seeing each other for two years. Michael had taken me to this gorgeous restaurant out on the water; the view was so breathtaking that you couldn't help from looking at it. I could remember clearly that there were these huge ships and small boats going by; the people that sailed them looked as though they were so relaxed and didn't have a worry in the world. For a moment I just wanted to feel the same peace and relaxation that they were feeling. When I felt this warm hand touch mine, reality kicked back in and there was Michael saying once again, "Would you marry me?"

Not that I didn't hear him the first time; I guess I wanted to block out the fact that he had asked me to marry him. I wasn't quite prepared for his proposal, so I took Michael's hands and took a deep breath and stared him directly in the eyes and answered him by saying, "No, I can't marry you! I'm sorry but I just don't want to get hurt anymore. I'm just too afraid to take another chance," so I quickly got up from the dinner table and walked away without looking back. I felt really bad about what I had done, but I just couldn't afford to risk my heart anymore. I heard Michael call out my name, but I kept right on walking as though I didn't hear him. When I arrived home, before I could even get in the door I could hear my telephone ringing off the hook. I looked at the caller ID and it read Michael. I didn't know whether to answer it or ignore it. I didn't want to hurt Michael anymore than I already had. I didn't know what to say to him; I wanted to convince myself that I was doing the right thing, but for some reason I just couldn't bring myself to feel that way. For a second, the phone had stopped ringing, but then it started ringing again. I knew that Michael would probably just keep right on calling me until I finally picked up the telephone. So I finally picked up the phone, and there was Michael, saying to me, "Are you all right? I hope I didn't upset you!"

I responded by saying, "No you didn't do anything wrong; I just wasn't expecting you to ask me those questions. They kind of caught me off guard."

Michael went on to say that if I needed more time to think things over, he would be patient while I did so. He said that he didn't want to lose me. I responded by saying, "Thank you for being understanding."

Michael answered back to me by saying, "You're welcome." Then the conversation ended.

Several weeks went by and I hadn't heard from Michael. I believed Michael had given me all the space that I needed. In fact, I was given so much space and time to think about things that I started to wonder if Michael ever did really exist in my world at all, or was he just an illusion of my imagination or something that I possibly created in my own mind after being hurt so many times. I thought Michael had totally forgotten about me, but who can blame him for not calling or coming by? I was very blunt about expressing my feelings toward him; after all, I probably made the man feel really bad about even proposing to me. But for God's sake, I was only being truthful about my feelings. It's not as if I sat there and planned out our evening by saying no. I didn't even see his proposal coming; it totally caught me off guard. One night while lying in my bed, I had this awful dream about Michael marrying another woman. She was beautiful and charming. The funny thing about my dream was that this woman whom he was going to marry was this woman I had never seen before. As they walked down the aisle before the preacher, side by side, waiting to be married to one another, Michael pulled up her veil, and the face I saw underneath the veil in my dream was me. I couldn't believe that I was seeing myself in my own dream. He took my hand and placed a ring on my finger, and all I could remember was him saying, "Until death do us part."

I woke up in a cold sweat, and all I could hear was my mother yelling out to me, "The telephone—it's Michael." My heart started to pound very quickly and I breathed a sigh of relief. I was just so happy to hear that Michael was still calling for me and that he hadn't given up on me. I was starting to become a little worried, and of course, the dream didn't make it any better. If anything, I believed it must have been a sign from God, trying to tell me that this man must be the man for me. So as I went to pick up the telephone, I said, "Hello?"

There was Michael saying, "Hello, I hope I didn't call too soon."

I said, "Oh no, actually I was just thinking about you. I'm glad you called. I need to see you, in person. There are some things I want to talk to you about."

Michael said, "Sure, when can we meet?"

I responded by saying, "At the restaurant you last proposed to me at."

Michael replied saying, "Are you sure that's a good idea?"

I responded saying, "I'm sure."

When we both hung up the phone, I sat up on my bed thinking about all the different ways I could tell Michael how sorry I was for turning down his proposal, and if it wasn't too late I would still love to accept his proposal. But I was afraid of what his response would be.

So the day came when Michael and I were at the restaurant where we both last had seen each other. There was Michael with his fine self, dressed up in a two-piece suit the color of burgundy; he was looking sharp as a tack. He smelled so good to me; all I could do was sniff at the air that surrounded him. I tried to keep my cool, but I so badly just wanted to grab this man and kiss him, and just spend my time making up for all the lost time spent apart. This time I found myself taking Michael by the hand and looking him in the eyes and asking him if he would still like to marry me, if, of course, he didn't have a change of heart.

Michael responded by saying, "No, I don't have a change of heart, and I would still love for you to become my wife. I was shocked that Michael still wanted to have me for his wife. I was just so happy, and grateful that I still had a chance to make this man my husband; after all, I did run off and leave him dateless.

Michael asked me when could we set a date to get married and I responded by saying, "Possibly in six months." He was delighted with my decision, so we both were very much looking forward to getting married.

One day while out shopping, Michael had mentioned to me that he ran into an old girlfriend of his from back in high school. He seemed very puzzled about how much this old girlfriend was so eager about getting together with him for old time's sake, she wanted to go out on a date with him. Michael said that he used to be in love with this old girlfriend of his, and hadn't seen her in about fifteen years. Michael also mentioned that she had broken his heart back in high school in order to date another man, whom she also knew from back in high school. But my Michael, being a decent man and all, said that he had forgiven her because they both were very young at the time. But Michael had also reassured me that he no longer had any feelings for this woman. He also told me how he had given her the rundown about us getting married in six months; how he was truly in love with me and my two kids. Michael didn't give her an answer right away; he told her that he first had to speak with me, to see if I was okay with him taking her out. But apparently this didn't make a difference to her. According to Michael, he said she still wouldn't give up on the idea of them still going out on a date together. Michael seemed to be more worried about how I felt; he didn't want to cause a problem by taking this ex-girlfriend of his out on a date. As I sat there listening to Michael run off at the mouth, I said to myself, "Just like Satan: ready to send a heffa along to try and mess up something that possibly God is trying to establish." But I learned as a little girl that when Satan would try to make an attack on me, I would simply rebuke and bind Satan in the name of Jesus. When Michael asked me if it was all right for them to go out on a supposedly innocent date, deep down inside I just wanted to yell out "Hell no!" But I had to be a bigger person than that, for I knew it was only a test that I was probably going through. I knew that I couldn't show any insecurity, because most men wouldn't find that attractive in a woman, especially one that they are about to marry. I said to myself, "Where the hell was this woman when I wasn't in the picture? Now all of a sudden she brings her beloved ass out of nowhere and wants to go on a date with my fiancé."

Michael said once again, "Are you okay with me taking her out on a date?"

I finally snapped back out of my deep thoughts, and answered Michael by saying,

"Sure, if you don't mind. What's the harm in two old friends going out on a date?"

Michael said, "Okay, well, I'll let her know that it's okay!" I just wanted to kick myself in the ass for keeping my cool through the whole thing. But I knew that it was just a matter of time before Michael and me would soon be married, and I had nothing to worry about. It was important that I show trust toward Michael, because if I didn't then what would be the point of us getting married?

The day had come when Michael and his old girlfriend did finally go out on a date. I was sure to mention to him that no matter where he decided to have dinner, just don't take her to our special place.

Michael answered me back by saying, "You have nothing to worry about; that particular restaurant belongs to us." That night I sat up in my living room, pacing the floor and looking at the clock, hoping he would walk in the door early saying that he had missed me and couldn't wait to get back to me. I just couldn't sleep so I turned on the TV to try and get my mind off the two of them. But that didn't work; for some reason, I just didn't have a good feeling about this old girlfriend of his. It's not as if I didn't trust my fiancé; I just didn't trust the woman he was dealing with. The reason for that was I couldn't understand why in the world this old girlfriend of his would want to be with a man from her past, when his heart was somewhere else. I thought to myself, "She must be desperate." I wouldn't have dared gone on a date with an ex-boyfriend of mine, especially with him being in love with another woman. I knew she was probably up to something, but I just couldn't put my finger on it. Later on that night, Michael came by my apartment. I could smell a little wine on his breath; also, I noticed a red smear of lipstick on his white-collared shirt. Boy! The things that started to run through my mind. I started to believe that something must have happened. There was Michael, looking as though he must have had a good time. I was just glad the whole dating thing was over with. I said to myself, "Hopefully this will be her first and her last date with Michael." I was just glad to have my man back again, and didn't want to share him with anyone else. I went on to ask Michael, "So how did things go with you and your old girlfriend?"

He answered by saying, "Okay, I guess."

I said to him, "What do you mean by okay?"

Michael answered by saying, "You know that I'm not big on drinking, but for some reason she felt offended if I didn't make a toast with her, for old time's sake. So I found myself drinking a glass of wine with her just because I didn't want her to feel any more out of place more than she already feels."

So I said to Michael, "What do you mean she feels out of place?"

He said, "You know, she felt bad once we arrived at dinner. She said she shouldn't have asked me out to dinner because now she feels foolish, knowing that I'm getting married soon."

So I said to Michael, "By the way, what's up with that smear of lipstick on your shirt? Did that have anything to do with the reason you were drinking against your will?"

Michael answered me as though he was shocked to see this lipstick mark on his shirt. He simply tried to explain to me that he must have rubbed up against his old girlfriend by accident. When Michael noticed that I wasn't buying his story, he finally admitted the truth to me.

"Okay! Okay! The truth is she tried to get me to kiss her when I took her home after dinner. But I pushed her away, and told her that I'm in love with my fiancée. So she quickly apologized and said she was sorry and ran into the house." I told Michael I knew she was up to something, but I just couldn't figure it out. Michael said to me, "Let's just put this whole thing behind us now."

So two months later, I get a knock on the door and there's this woman looking like she just lost her best friend, crying and demanding to speak with my man. I'm like, "Who are you? What do you want with Michael?" She responded by saying that she needed to speak with him about something really important. I said, "Whatever it is, you can tell me. I'm his fiancée." So she went on to say that she went to the doctor this morning and found out she was two months' pregnant, and she believed that Michael was the father of her unborn child.

I couldn't believe what I was hearing; I just wanted this whole thing to be a nightmare. I said to this strange woman, "How did you know where I lived?" She answered me by saying that she was the old girlfriend that went out on a date with Michael, and she had followed him home one night to see where he was staying. I said to myself, "Another fatal attraction on the loose." Once again she demanded to see Michael, and I told her for the last time that he wasn't home and to please not bring that momma's-drama-pappa-maybe stuff around my house anymore.

Well, this old girlfriend of Michael's just stood there and rolled her eyes at me and sucked her teeth, and said while walking away, "Just please give Michael my message." I slammed the front door as hard as I could, hoping that she got the message that she was no longer welcome on my porch or to my home anymore.

When Michael arrived at my place later on that evening, boy was I furious! I was going to let him have it. Michael walked in the door whistling as though he had a good day. I said to myself, "Only when he hears what I have to say." Michael came up to me and gave me a hug and a kiss and asked me how was my day, and I responded by saying, "Not so good. You know, that old girlfriend of yours came by here crying and demanding to speak with you."

Michael said, "I wonder why."

I then said to Michael, "So that explains why there was lipstick on your shirt and wine on your breath."

Michael said, "So what are you trying to say?"

Then I responded by saying, "She said that she's two months' pregnant, and the baby is supposedly yours."

Michael looked at me in total shock; he said to me that he never touched that woman. "What does she mean, I'm the father? I never even kissed her, let alone had sex with her." Michael said she was lying, and now he regretted taking her out on a date. He also mentioned that he shouldn't have forgiven her so easily back in high school. He said he thought that she had changed and matured, but he guessed he was wrong about her. Michael then took me by the hands and looked me in my eyes with a serious look like I'd never seen before. He said to me, "Baby, you have to believe me. I'm telling you the truth. I would never do anything that foolish to jeopardize our relationship. I love you too much to lose you over something like this."

I then knew that I needed to give Michael the benefit of the doubt. I didn't want to just say that I felt he was lying, so I told Michael I just wanted to be alone for a little while so that I could think about things and try to make sense of everything that was going on. He wasn't too happy about giving me my space; he wanted to stay with me and talk some more. But he knew that would have just made me more upset. I just needed a little more time to figure out why someone would want to make up a story like that for no good reason. Well, two days later, there was Michael at my door, bright and early, with two cups of coffee and danishes. I had just gotten out of bed when I went to open the door.

"Good morning," Michael said. I said good morning back. Then he came up to me like he usually did and gave me a big hug and kiss. He sat down on the couch and I sat down beside him, hoping to not start my day off by talking about his old girlfriend. Michael grabbed the remote control and turned on the television. He always liked to watch the news; he felt if he didn't keep up with the news, he was out of the loop about things at work. All of a sudden there came this important news flash about a serious accident that had taken place on a major highway. They showed faces of the victims that were injured very badly, and what did we happen to see? Michael's old girlfriend on the news flash.

Michael overheard the news reporter saying that the victims involved in the terrible car accident were rushed to Baystate Medical Hospital. We both jumped up and rushed on over to the hospital, without thinking twice about what just happened a couple of days ago. We felt it was our chance to find out the truth about this ex-girlfriend of his, if she really was pregnant.

How I've Grown to Know True Love

Once we arrived, Michael went up to the doctor and mentioned that he knew a particular person that had been injured in the accident, and that he was the father of her unborn child. The doctor said that she had lost a lot of blood and was unconscious, but she had been given a blood transfusion and was going to be all right. Michael then asked the doctor if the baby she was carrying okay. The doctor looked at both of us in a state of shock and said, "What baby? There were never any indications of her being pregnant."

After that day at the hospital, I knew never to doubt my fiancé again. Shortly thereafter, Michael and I moved on with our lives, putting the past behind us. Our wedding day finally arrived; we had a big church wedding with lots of friends and family. We bought this big beautiful house and made it into a loving home. Then we both were blessed with two little girls.

I forgot to mention my two sons, of course. Since then, we have been happily married. This is my story about "how I've grown to know true love."

The End.

ABOUT THE AUTHOR

My name is Terry La-shon Riley. I was born May 29, 1970, in Newark, New Jersey. I grew up as a Baptist; I attended a Baptist church in East Orange, New Jersey. I was raised by my mother, Alberta Williams, and stepfather, Frank Williams. I'm also the youngest sibling out of my mother's four children. I graduated in 1988 from Plainfield High School in Plainfield, New Jersey, where I received my high school diploma. . I attended Phillips Business School, in 1989, in East Orange, New Jersey, where I received a certificate in Business Courses and WordPerfect 5.0. A few years later I moved to the state of Massachusetts, where I attended Greenfield Community College. There I majored in social work. I'm currently a wife, the mother of four kids, and a daycare provider, who works out of her own home with children. What interested me as an author were my life experiences, the ups and downs, which gave me the strength to write about the many challenges that I had dealt with in life. I'm just proud to say that through it all was a brighter side waiting for me!

Printed in the United States
49410LVS00001B/322-366